Alive in the WORD

CLOUD OF WITNESSES

I0792877

PAUL

Pastoring God's People

John W. Martens

Little Rock Scripture Study

A ministry of the Diocese of Little Rock
in partnership with Liturgical Press

Nihil obstat: Jerome Kodell, OSB, *Censor Librorum.*
Imprimatur: ✠ Anthony B. Taylor, Bishop of Little Rock, April 19, 2018.

Cover design by Ann Blattner. Cover photo: Getty Images. Used with permission.

Photos/illustrations: Pages 6, 18, 20, 24, 29, 31, 37, Getty Images. Used with permission. Page 13, Clifford M. Yeary.

 Published by Liturgical Press, Collegeville, Minnesota 56321. Printed in the United States of America.

Library of Congress Control Number: 2017958486

ISBN: 978-0-8146-4506-2 (print); 978-0-8146-4530-7 (e-book)

Contents

Introduction

Alive in the Word brings you resources to deepen your understanding of Scripture, offer meaning for your life today, and help you to pray and act in response to God's word.

Use any volume of **Alive in the Word** in the way best suited to you.

- **For individual learning and reflection,** consider this an invitation to prayerfully journal in response to the questions you find along the way. And be prepared to move from head to heart and then to action.
- **For group learning and reflection**, arrange for three sessions where you will use the material provided as the basis for faith sharing and prayer. You may ask group members to read each chapter in advance and come prepared with questions answered. In this kind of session, plan to be together for about an hour. Or, if your group prefers, read and respond to the questions together without advance preparation. With this approach, it's helpful to plan on spending more time for each group session in order to adequately work through each of the chapters.

- **For a parish-wide event or use within a larger group,** provide each person with a copy of this volume, and allow time during the event for quiet reading, group discussion and prayer, and then a final commitment by each person to some simple action in response to what he or she learned.

This volume on the topic of Paul emphasizes his pastoral character and is one of several volumes dedicated to **Cloud of Witnesses.** The pages of our Bibles are filled with the stories of women and men who have played a unique role in salvation history. By entering into a few key biblical passages written by or describing these people, we begin to see how our own story continues God's great work of salvation in the world. Their witness, handed on to us from centuries ago, continues to speak to us and challenge us to stand as faithful witnesses in today's world.

Faith, Hope, and Love

Begin by asking God to assist you in your prayer and study. Then read through 1 Thessalonians 1:2-10, the thanksgiving of Paul's First Letter to the Thessalonians.

1 Thessalonians 1:2-10

[2] We give thanks to God always for all of you, remembering
you in our prayers, unceasingly [3] calling to mind your work
of faith and labor of love and endurance in hope of our Lord
Jesus Christ, before our God and Father, [4] knowing, brothers
loved by God, how you were chosen. [5] For our gospel did not
come to you in word alone, but also in power and in the holy
Spirit and [with] much conviction. You know what sort of
people we were [among] you for your sake. [6] And you became

imitators of us and of the Lord, receiving the word in great affliction, with joy from the holy Spirit, [7] so that you became a model for all the believers in Macedonia and in Achaia. [8] For from you the word of the Lord has sounded forth not only in Macedonia and [in] Achaia, but in every place your faith in God has gone forth, so that we have no need to say anything. [9] For they themselves openly declare about us what sort of reception we had among you, and how you turned to God from idols to serve the living and true God [10] and to await his Son from heaven, whom he raised from [the] dead, Jesus, who delivers us from the coming wrath.

After a few moments of quiet reflection on the passage from Paul's First Letter to the Thessalonians, consider the background information provided in "Setting the Scene."

Setting the Scene

Paul's First Letter to the Thessalonians is the earliest written document found in the New Testament, having been composed and sent in 49–50 AD. Paul traveled to Thessalonica with Timothy and Barnabas to bring the message of Jesus and to found a church not long before the letter was written. Paul's mission to Thessalonica is described in Acts 17 where we learn that Paul and his coworkers had to leave the city under duress as a mob formed by some of the locals from the *agora*, or marketplace, were after them. When they could not find Paul or his companions, they began to persecute some of the local disciples.

Paul sent this letter, as he did all of his letters, to check in with the church in Thessalonica and to build them up as disciples of Jesus. Paul describes himself in this letter as both the father and the mother of the Thessalonians, who nursed them in their faith and encouraged them to grow in holiness. He also speaks of his anxiety for these new Christians, as he was concerned they might abandon their faith due to the persecution they had experienced. But Timothy had gone back to visit them, bringing Paul's letter with him, and brought back news of the steadfastness of the Thessalonians.

The goal of the pastor is to build up the congregation. When has a pastor or someone else encouraged you, as an individual and as a part of the Body of Christ, to remain faithful in terms of persecution or distress?

Paul spends much of the letter exhorting the Thessalonians to live holy lives and explaining basic theological concepts, such as the *parousia*, or "Second Coming," of Jesus. In the passage we are studying, known as the "thanksgiving," which occurs right after the salutation, or opening of the letter, Paul does indeed give thanks for the Christian community in Thessalonica and describes how they came to be Christians and how they have persevered in the faith in spite of the suffering they have experienced. It is important to remember that the Thessalonians are mostly former pagans, who have no Gospels to consult and no established church hierarchy beyond the apostles. As a result, any theological questions they need answered or any difficulties they are experiencing require Paul's intervention. Paul is not only the missionary who founded the church in Thessalonica, he is the pastor who shepherds, guides, protects, and encourages his flock.

Understanding the Scene Itself

> *The entire passage will be considered a few verses at a time. The occasional questions in the margin (as above) are for discussion with others. If you are using these materials on your own, use the questions for personal reflection or as a guide to journaling.*

**2 We give thanks to God always for all of you,
remembering you in our prayers, unceasingly
3 calling to mind your work of faith and labor
of love and endurance in hope of our Lord Jesus
Christ, before our God and Father, 4 knowing,
brothers loved by God, how you were chosen.**

A key part of a Hellenistic letter is known as the "thanksgiving" in which the author offers thanks and warm wishes and sets the stage for the rest of the letter. Because Paul's letters are a part of his authoritative apostolic presence, his thanksgiving contains his hopes for the Christian communities to whom he is writing and often an outline of what he will cover in the rest of the letter.

Do you give thanks regularly to people in your life, whether it is in a spiritual context or just the run of daily life?

Paul, who writes this letter with Timothy and Barnabas, tells the congregation that they—the "you" throughout the thanksgiving is in plural in Greek—are mentioned in prayer always. That is common for Paul's thanksgivings. What is remarkable is that Paul notes that he and his coworkers remember the faith, love, and hope the Thessalonians have in "our Lord Jesus Christ." In the first Christian document, Paul mentions

***agapē* = self-sacrificing love**

***pistis* = trust-filled faith**

***elpis* = supernatural hope in God**

what will become known in the Christian tradition as the three theological virtues. Love is *agapē*, a self-sacrificing love, in which one looks out for and cares for the needs of others. Faith is *pistis*, more than simply an intellectual belief in something, it is the trust of the whole person in God and in God's promises. Hope is *elpis*, which refers to the supernatural hope in God and God's promises.

How do you show faith, hope, and love in your life? Do you struggle with one of the virtues more than the others?

In addition to naming these three theological virtues, which are to characterize all Christians, Paul names the means by which we are to gain and grow in them: "work of faith," "labor of love," and "steadfastness of hope." Note that "work" (*ergon*), "labor" (*kopos*), and "endurance" (*hypomonē*) all reflect the sort of perseverance and steadfastness necessary to grow in the theological virtues. Pope Benedict XVI, in fact, in his encyclical letter *Spe Salvi*, reflects on *hypomonē*. He states it is "knowing how to wait, while patiently enduring trials" and "in the religious context of ancient Judaism, this word was used expressly for the expectation of God which was characteristic of Israel, for their persevering faithfulness to God on the basis of the certainty of the Covenant," which acquires a new certainty in the revelation of Christ (9). To live in the virtues, work, labor, and steadfastness are needed.

Is there an area of your life where work, labor, and endurance are needed?

Paul also tells the Thessalonians that they were "chosen" (*eklogē*) by God. When Paul uses this word *eklogē*, it points not only to God's choosing them, but to the fact that the Thessalonians, like us, have responded to God's call by accepting it and living according to the call.

[5] For our gospel did not come to you in word
alone, but also in power and in the holy Spirit
and [with] much conviction. You know what
sort of people we were [among] you for your
sake. [6] And you became imitators of us and of
the Lord, receiving the word in great affliction,
with joy from the holy Spirit, [7] so that you be-
came a model for all the believers in Macedonia
and in Achaia.

Paul certainly understands that to be "chosen" means to live out the baptismal call, for he speaks of the Gospel (*euangelion*) coming not in "word alone," in the spoken preaching of Paul, Barnabas, and Timothy, but in "power" (*dynamis*)—the word from which we get the English "dynamite"—and in the Holy Spirit "with much conviction." This points to the Holy Spirit-filled manner in which Paul delivered the Gospel to the Thessalonians, and also their willingness to be open to the Holy Spirit working in and through them with power.

When have you felt the power of the Holy Spirit working in you or your parish community?

Finally, Paul points to the type of people Paul and his coworkers "proved to be" among the Thessalonians. Later in the letter (2:3-8), Paul explains again that he had come not to make money from them and that he left due to persecution, but that his only goal was to bring the Thessalonians the saving message of Jesus. In a world in which *sophists* travelled from city to city making money by fawning over the inhabitants and speaking flattering words, Paul says that Christian pastors are there to serve the people and to be there for "their sake."

Paul's claim that the Thessalonians "became imitators of us and of the Lord" is significant in an ancient Greco-Roman context. "Imitation" (*mimēsis*) was not considered a form of flattery or lack of originality, but the way in which a child or disciple modeled themselves on their superiors, such as a parent or a teacher. The qualities that people manifest are the things that we most often imitate. For the spiritual children of Paul the pastor, and he refers to himself as both the mother and father of the Thessalonians (2:7, 11-12), the apostle was someone whom it was necessary to "imitate" in order to grow to spiritual maturity.

Are there particular people, priests, sisters, deacons, family members, or friends, you have as models of imitation in your Christian journey? How have they helped you along the path?

The Thessalonians are imitators of both Paul and Jesus because they remained faithful to Jesus Christ, "with joy from the holy Spirit," even though at such an early point in their faith life, they suffered persecution. Some scholars think that a later discussion in 1 Thessalonians 4:13, about some of the Thessalonians who have died ("fallen asleep"), might indicate that some members of the church were killed in the initial persecution. Their steadfast faith in this suffering, says Paul, "became a model for all the believers in Macedonia and [in] Achaia." When we live out our faith, even to martyrdom in some cases, it does draw people to the living hope of Jesus Christ and models the love that Paul reports among the Thessalonians.

[8] **For from you the word of the Lord has sounded forth not only in Macedonia and [in] Achaia, but in every place your faith in God has gone forth, so that we have no need to say anything. [9] For they themselves openly declare about us what sort of reception we had among you, and how you turned to God from idols to serve the living and true God [10] and to await his Son from heaven, whom he raised from [the] dead, Jesus, who delivers us from the coming wrath.**

Even at this early stage of Christian growth and development, the word about the small church in Thessalonica has spread beyond the two Greek provinces of Macedonia and Achaia to the rest of the churches in the Roman Empire. In a world in which travel took much longer than today, on foot, donkey, or on ships, Paul claims that "in every place your faith in God has gone forth." People are drawn

to and want to imitate the powerful witness of faith lived in love.

The Thessalonians have also gained renown, says Paul, for welcoming Paul, Barnabas, and Timothy. More significantly, that welcome included turning from idols "to serve the living and true God." We must keep in mind that the ancient world was not a world without gods, but a world full of gods. For people to turn to the one God was to turn their backs on family and city gods and even the growing worship of the emperor at this point in history. The Thessalonian Christians, that is, had to make a choice to be potentially cut off from their kinship and extended networks to be disciples of Jesus. They were all in.

What gods do you notice drawing people away from Christ today? Who is a model for you in drawing people to the living and true God?

Why could they make such a powerful decision even in the face of the cost of losing friends and family, perhaps employment, and even their lives? A part of Paul's pastoring was to teach his congregations that Jesus would return "from heaven" where he dwelt since he was resurrected from the dead. The whole notion of resurrection would have been new to the Thessalonians, since Greco-Roman religion believed in life continuing on as an immortal soul or as shades in Hades. Christians, however, like most Jews (the Sadducees were a notable exception), understood that the whole person, body and soul, would be raised to live in the presence of God for eternity. The Thessalonians were convinced of the resurrection and Jesus' return. It was not as if the present world did not matter to them as Christians, but that they had reoriented their hope toward eternity.

When Paul notes that Jesus "delivers us from the coming wrath," he is referencing the whole range of apocalyptic ideas that are sometimes troubling to modern readers. Yet, we must remember that this was at the heart of Jesus' teaching as well as Paul's. Ideas of the Apocalypse form the backdrop for the understanding of the resurrection, namely, that at the end of time God will act to conquer evil and establish God's kingdom. Modern thinkers, as well as ancient and medieval ones, have sometimes taken it upon themselves to try to fix or prophesy the coming of the end, something that Jesus tells us cannot be done (see Mark 13:32-33; Acts 1:7). Current-day apocalyptic prophets might embarrass us, but this teaching is at the heart of biblical revelation as well as the Nicene Creed: "He will come again in glory to judge the living and the dead and his kingdom will have no end." "The wrath," therefore, that Paul speaks of is separation from the presence of God for eternity. Those who belong to Jesus will be saved from darkness to live with Jesus in eternity. The path to eternity is not about predicting the time of the end, but about *living as Christian witnesses in faith, hope, and love.*

Praying the Word / Sacred Reading

Return to the passage in 1 Thessalonians 1:2-10, reading it slowly and prayerfully. Consider what words or phrases stand out for you and spend some time reflecting on why these words are speaking to you. Try to imagine yourself as a recipient of this letter from Paul in the first century in Thessalonica. Consider how God is speaking to you.

If you are sharing this with a group, allow for some time to read the passage silently. At that point you might want one person to read the reflections below while the others consider the questions quietly. Then take time to talk about the various pieces of the passage that stand out for you.

You have tried your best to follow Jesus Christ as Paul, Barnabas, and Timothy showed you. But Paul had to leave when persecution came and the whole community suffered. You wondered whether God cared for you or whether Paul even remembered you. But Timothy came with a letter written by Paul and your heart has been strengthened by your pastor's words.

Now, you recall again the power of the Holy Spirit working in your life and the life of the Church. Have you been open to letting the Spirit work in you? Have you been listening for the Spirit?

Paul has also talked about the faith, love, and hope of your community. You wonder, have you allowed these virtues to grow in you? Have you always maintained faith? Have you ever lost hope? Have you ever acted without love? Pray that God might strengthen you.

Sometimes the things of this world pull you away from God and from the hope of Jesus' return, from the salvation that Paul spoke of in Christ Jesus. You ask for the power and the strength to place your hope not in the things of this world, but to shape your life in imitation of Paul and especially of Jesus. You pray for your church, for your pastor, and for yourself that you might always witness to the hope, faith, and love of Jesus.

Living the Word

Consider how you might demonstrate the Christian virtues of faith, hope, and love in your family, at work, among friends, or even while you are out driving or shopping.

- *How can you continue to show God's love?*
- *What would be a concrete demonstration of hope that transcends even the sufferings of this world?*
- *In what way could you show your faith?*

Think about how you have been helped to grow in these ways by your spiritual guides, pastors, and others, and how you might be able to pastor others in the theological virtues. Can you think today about someone who needs to encounter the love, faith, and hope found in God?

You Are the Body of Christ

Begin by asking God to assist you in your prayer and study. Then read through 1 Corinthians 12:12-31, a part of Paul's encouragement to the Corinthians to recognize their own spiritual gifts and to value each other's spiritual gifts.

1 Corinthians 12:12-31

12 As a body is one though it
has many parts, and all the
parts of the body, though
many, are one body, so also
Christ. 13 For in one Spirit we
were all baptized into one body,
whether Jews or Greeks, slaves or free
persons, and we were all given to drink of one Spirit.
14 Now the body is not a single part, but many. 15 If a foot
should say, "Because I am not a hand I do not belong to the
body," it does not for this reason belong any less to the body.
16 Or if an ear should say, "Because I am not an eye I do not
belong to the body," it does not for this reason belong any
less to the body. 17 If the whole body were an eye, where would
the hearing be? If the whole body were hearing, where would
the sense of smell be? 18 But as it is, God placed the parts,
each one of them, in the body as he intended. 19 If they were
all one part, where would the body be? 20 But as it is, there

are many parts, yet one body. [21] The eye cannot
say to the hand, "I do not need you," nor again
the head to the feet, "I do not need you." [22] In-
deed, the parts of the body that seem to be
weaker are all the more necessary, [23] and those
parts of the body that we consider less honorable
we surround with greater honor, and our less
presentable parts are treated with greater pro-
priety, [24] whereas our more presentable parts do
not need this. But God has so constructed the
body as to give greater honor to a part that is
without it, [25] so that there may be no division in
the body, but that the parts may have the same
concern for one another. [26] If [one] part suffers,
all the parts suffer with it; if one part is honored,
all the parts share its joy.
[27] Now you are Christ's body, and individually
parts of it. [28] Some people God has designated
in the church to be, first, apostles; second,
prophets; third, teachers; then, mighty deeds;
then, gifts of healing, assistance, administration,
and varieties of tongues. [29] Are all apostles? Are
all prophets? Are all teachers? Do all work
mighty deeds? [30] Do all have gifts of healing? Do
all speak in tongues? Do all interpret? [31] Strive
eagerly for the greatest spiritual gifts.

But I shall show you a still more excellent way.

After a few moments of quiet reflection on the passage from Paul's First Letter to the Corinthians, consider the background information provided in "Setting the Scene." Questions in the margin are for your reflection and/or group discussion.

Setting the Scene

Paul had a complex relationship with the church in Corinth, existing in a cosmopolitan port city, the capitol of the Roman senatorial province of Achaia. Located on the isthmus that connected the Peloponnese peninsula to mainland Greece, it was situated between the Adriatic Sea to the west and the Aegean Sea to the east. It was a significant seaport and a natural trading center between east and west. The city was associated with vice, especially sexual vice. The Temple of Aphrodite might have housed up to one thousand prostitutes, the majority of them slaves. The city was also noted for its religious syncretism, and the skyline was dominated by the Temple of Aphrodite on the Acrocorinth to the south and the Temple of Apollo in the middle of the city. It was also home to a synagogue, and fragments of the stone inscription "Synagogue of the Hebrews" have been found in the ancient ruins.

The Corinthian church was founded when Paul arrived after leaving Athens around 49 AD (Acts 18:1-18). He was later joined by Silvanus and Timothy. Paul first taught in the synagogue and then in a Greek convert's home. He stayed at least eighteen months in Corinth, and perhaps even longer. According to Paul's own letter to the Corinthians, he supported himself during this time by his work as a tentmaker (1 Cor 9:6).

Paul's situation with the Corinthians was complex on many levels; we know believers in Corinth misunderstood or misinterpreted a number of things Paul said. They had divided into factions, aligning themselves with Paul, Apollos, or Peter (Cephas). Some people also thought that Paul had disallowed marriage, while other people were visiting prostitutes or, in the case of one man, living with his stepmother. There were also problems with some people claiming spiritual superiority, a division that spilled over into the Eucharistic assemblies and *led to drunkenness during their worship*.

These issues were not all solved by 1 Corinthians as Paul's authority was later challenged by interlopers into the community, people whom Paul calls in 2 Corinthians "false" or "super" apostles. The Corinthians seem not to have always accepted Paul's authority as an apostle and they accused him of being weak in speech and/or presence. Paul claims that weakness, such as suffering for Christ, is what true apostles and disciples do. He claims that the Corinthians are children in the faith even though they claim to be spiritually mature. He challenges them here

Growing in faith is essential for each of us. In which areas have you grown in faith? What areas still call out for growth and maturity?

How has a pastor, friend, or spiritual guide persevered in guiding you?

to understand that they are one body, all essential parts of the Body of Christ.

Generally it is thought that 1 Corinthians was written in 54 AD, but this was not Paul's first letter to the community; he speaks in 1 Corinthians 5:9 of an earlier letter sent to the church. So, 1 Corinthians is (at least) the second letter that Paul has sent to them. We also know that the Corinthians were in contact with Paul via visits from some church members (1:11) and a letter they sent to Paul (7:1). We know that the issues were unresolved when Paul sent 2 Corinthians. Indeed, from internal evidence in 2 Corinthians, it is believed that it is either Paul's fourth or fifth letter to Corinth! One thing we know is that a pastor must persevere, and Paul, as the spiritual father of the Corinthians, was not willing to give up on his spiritual children!

> *The entire passage will be considered a few verses at a time to explore valuable lessons more carefully.*

Understanding the Scene Itself

[12] As a body is one though it has many parts, and all the parts of the body, though many, are one body, so also Christ. [13] For in one Spirit we were all baptized into one body, whether Jews or Greeks, slaves or free persons, and we were all given to drink of one Spirit.

Paul calls the church in Corinth, and its members, the "body" (*sōma*) of Christ, the same word used in Greek for the physical body. A physical body has many parts, but all are united in the functioning of the whole. This is a beautiful image which may even have emerged for Paul in his conversion experience on the road to Damascus because Jesus states that Paul in persecuting the disciples of Jesus is actually persecuting him (Acts 9:4-5). It is possible that in Paul's Damascus road experience, he came to recognize that all Christians were joined together as part of Christ's body.

How have you experienced the church as the Body of Christ?

For Paul, this is more than a metaphor. He develops the image of the "one body" by saying that everyone who has been baptized is *baptized into the one body through the one Spirit, which transcends ethnic or social divisions*. If all Christians are a part of one body of Christ, there ought to be no divisions among us. This was difficult to live out in antiquity, as it is today. Apart from major divisions among Christians historically and today, we can find small ones in our individual congregations, just as we see in Corinth.

Where have you noticed problems of division in your parish or local church community? Are there ways in which you have acted or could act to increase a sense of unity in the church?

14 Now the body is not a single part, but many.
15 If a foot should say, "Because I am not a hand
I do not belong to the body," it does not for this
reason belong any less to the body. 16 Or if an
ear should say, "Because I am not an eye I do
not belong to the body," it does not for this
reason belong any less to the body. 17 If the
whole body were an eye, where would the hear-
ing be? If the whole body were hearing, where

would the sense of smell be? [18] But as it is, God placed the parts, each one of them, in the body as he intended. [19] If they were all one part, where would the body be? [20] But as it is, there are many parts, yet one body. [21]The eye cannot say to the hand, "I do not need you," nor again the head to the feet, "I do not need you."

Are there times you have felt insignificant within the church, in the broader community, or even in your family?

What has helped you feel an important part of the Body of Christ?

If you do not yet feel a significant part, could you find a guide in your parish or among your friends and family with whom you could speak?

Paul's extended analogy of the body being made up of many parts is simple and straightforward, but the power of it is sometimes overlooked. When we look at our own roles or those of others we may feel we have little power or significance. But every part of the body has a role to play that only it can play. The apostle stresses that each person is fundamental to the Body of Christ no matter how insignificant they might appear in the world or even within the church. For the whole of the body to function smoothly, every person is necessary, including children, the elderly, those who are disabled, and those who are ill. There are no unnecessary parts in the Body of Christ.

22 Indeed, the parts of the body that seem to be
weaker are all the more necessary, 23 and those
parts of the body that we consider less honorable
we surround with greater honor, and our less
presentable parts are treated with greater pro-
priety, 24 whereas our more presentable parts do
not need this. But God has so constructed the
body as to give greater honor to a part that is
without it, 25 so that there may be no division in
the body, but that the parts may have the same
concern for one another. 26 If [one] part suffers,
all the parts suffer with it; if one part is honored,
all the parts share its joy.

There is a fascinating claim that Paul makes in which he states, "the parts of the body that seem to be weaker are all the more necessary." In fact, he maintains his analogy about the body to say that those body parts deemed weaker are surrounded and protected in order to give them greater honor. It is possible that Paul points here to the protection of the "little ones," the children, the weak, and the marginalized, so often praised in the teachings of Jesus (e.g., Matt 18:1-10; 19:4).

It also helps make sense of the fact that if one part of the body suffers, all do, so to pretend that it does not matter if a weaker member of the body is injured or harmed, while someone powerful and strong is thriving, is wrong. We are all in this together: children, clergy, parents, single people, the poor and the rich.

How have you reached out to those in greater need of support and affirmation? In what ways have you helped others recognize their significance for the Body of Christ? How can you help them recognize their talents?

27 Now you are Christ's body, and individually
parts of it. 28 Some people God has designated

in the church to be, first, apostles; second, prophets; third, teachers; then, mighty deeds; then, gifts of healing, assistance, administration, and varieties of tongues. [29] Are all apostles? Are all prophets? Are all teachers? Do all work mighty deeds? [30] Do all have gifts of healing? Do all speak in tongues? Do all interpret? [31] Strive eagerly for the greatest spiritual gifts.

But I shall show you a still more excellent way.

The fact that we are all the Body of Christ means that each of us has specific roles, whether they are formal—priest, religious sister, deacon, or lay ecclesial minister—or informal—the cheerful parishioner who greets everyone warmly, or the person who comes to daily Mass. Paul does speak, though, of particular gifts and offices in the church. These religious gifts take many forms and Paul asks that each of us develop our gifts, whatever they might be.

Are you still identifying your gifts? Are you working on sharing them with the broader community?

Paul identifies many spiritual gifts and, as a good pastor, encourages everyone to seek the greatest gifts. Suddenly, though, he says he will show us "a still more excellent way." The "more excellent way" that Paul identifies also as the greatest spiritual gift is love (1 Cor 13). Love is a gift that all are able to share in and share with others, regardless of age, status, or condition. Paul draws us back again to the unity of the body. Though we have many talents and skills, unique to each of us, and many offices and positions, and many spiritual gifts, what binds us together as the Body of Christ is love.

Of the three theological virtues—faith, hope, and love—only love lasts eternally (1 Cor 13:13) and is the greatest gift of all. How are you sharing your love with all? Are you able to accept love from others?

Praying the Word / Sacred Reading

Return to the passage in 1 Corinthians 12:12-31, reading it slowly and prayerfully. Consider what words or phrases stand out for you and spend some time reflecting on why these words are speaking to you. You might want to envision yourself as a recipient of this letter from Paul in the first century in Corinth. But you might also place yourself in your own situation today.

If you are sharing this with a group allow for some time to read the passage silently. At that point you might want one person to read the reflections below while the others consider the questions quietly. Then take time to talk about the various pieces of the passage that stand out for you.

> It can be difficult if you feel you do not have a role in your community or if you feel that your role is not valued, whether in the first or twenty-first century. If you are troubled by a sense of not knowing your place or not feeling valued, think about your spiritual gifts and the skills and abilities that you bring to your community. When have you felt that you were contributing most to your parish, friends, workplace, community, school, or family?
>
> Think about the joy you have felt in giving of your gifts to others. What allowed you to unlock and share those gifts? Is there something you can do to grow in your gifts?

Is there someone you can speak to in order to help you grow in these gifts?

Paul has also spoken about everyone having a role or a place in the Body of Christ. Is there some way for you to help others grasp their own gifts?

Love, Paul says, is that gift that all have and which draws us nearer and nearer to God since God is love. Pray for the greatest gift of all, for you, for your family, friends, and fellow parishioners. Remember, your pastor and others have formal roles in the Body of Christ, but all of us are necessary for the thriving of the body. Pray that your parish and that the church as a whole might see that love is the path to unity and to the recognition of our shared and essential gifts.

Living the Word

What might be the best way for you to demonstrate that we are all in the church the Body of Christ and that we all have important contributions to make to the whole body? Are there concrete ways for you to demonstrate acceptance of someone with whom you have been at odds? Is there a way to open doors for others or yourself to serve the church with all of your gifts?

Pray that you might be able to serve to help create unity and not factions or divisions, even at a small level, within the church. Paul gave us the analogy of the body for a reason, so how do we keep the body healthy and vigorous?

Live by the Spirit

Begin by asking God to assist you in your prayer and study. Then read through Galatians 5:13-26, in which Paul urges the Galatians to live by the Spirit and not by the flesh.

Galatians 5:13-26
13 For you were called for freedom, brothers. But do not use
this freedom as an opportunity for the flesh; rather, serve one
another through love. 14 For the whole law is fulfilled in one
statement, namely, "You shall love your neighbor as yourself."
15 But if you go on biting and devouring one another, beware
that you are not consumed by one another.
16 I say, then: live by the Spirit and you will certainly not grat-
ify the desire of the flesh. 17 For the flesh has desires against the
Spirit, and the Spirit against the flesh; these are opposed to
each other, so that you may not do what you want. 18 But if
you are guided by the Spirit, you are not under the law. 19 Now
the works of the flesh are obvious: immorality, impurity, li-
centiousness, 20 idolatry, sorcery, hatreds, rivalry, jealousy, out-
bursts of fury, acts of selfishness, dissensions, factions,
21 occasions of envy, drinking bouts, orgies, and the like. I warn

you, as I warned you before, that those who do
such things will not inherit the kingdom of God.
22 In contrast, the fruit of the Spirit is love, joy,
peace, patience, kindness, generosity, faithfulness,
23 gentleness, self-control. Against such there is
no law. 24 Now those who belong to Christ [Jesus]
have crucified their flesh with its passions and
desires. 25 If we live in the Spirit, let us also follow
the Spirit. 26 Let us not be conceited, provoking
one another, envious of one another.

After a few moments of quiet reflection on the passage from Paul's letter to the Galatians, consider the background information provided in "Setting the Scene."

Setting the Scene

Paul's letter is directed "to the churches of the Galatians," that is, Paul is writing to a number of congregations he has founded that all seem to be struggling with similar issues. While scholars have wrestled with whether the recipients are located in the Roman province of Galatia, whose mission is described especially in Acts 13:14–14:23, or to the actual Celtic tribes, namely Gauls who emigrated to Asia Minor in the third century BC, that is not a major concern for understanding the letter.

Both Galatians 1:6-9 and 3:1-5 indicate that Paul founded the churches in Galatia. For instance, in Galatians 3:2, Paul writes, "the only thing I want to learn from you is this: Did you receive the Spirit by doing the works of the law or by believing what you heard?" This references the initial Galatian acceptance of the Gospel in the Holy Spirit when Paul was first among them and gives an indication as to why he is so upset that they appear to be abandoning the Gospel.

In this letter, Paul is perhaps more frustrated than in any other of his writings—it is Paul's only letter in which he does not offer a thanksgiving! Paul is passionately and sometimes angrily defending the Gospel and his ministry to the Galatians. There are clearly "opponents" whom Paul is addressing, people who have come into the Galatian churches from the "outside" (Gal 4:16-17, 5:10, 12). These people have come to the Galatian churches arguing that the observance of the Law of Moses is necessary for salvation; the shorthand for this in Paul's letter is "circumcision."

Paul takes a harsh tone with the Galatians. Are there times when sharp criticism of your life or choices was necessary for you to get back on track in living out the Gospel? Have there been times when criticism harmed or scarred you? Do you welcome praise when you have turned your life around?

Without question these opponents were, like Paul himself, Jewish Christians, but these Jewish Christians believed that it was still essential that all Christians, Jewish or Gentile, continue to follow the Law of Moses in every respect. They also attempt to discredit Paul himself as an apostle, which is why Paul finds it essential to defend not just his Gospel but himself (Gal 1:1, 11-12). Paul denies that by arguing for the sufficiency of Christ he is at odds with God's promises to the Jewish people, since Paul sees Christ as the one who fulfills all of God's promises. In this letter Paul the pastor struggles to bring his congregations to a true understanding of salvation in Christ.

The entire passage will be considered a few verses at a time. The occasional questions in the margin will help guide your study and reflection.

Understanding the Scene Itself

13 For you were called for freedom, brothers. But do not use this freedom as an opportunity for the flesh; rather, serve one another through love.

In this verse Paul addresses the ethical implications of freedom in Christ. What does it mean to live free from the Law? Paul does not put this in negative form; he positively asks what it means to be "called to freedom." Freedom is an "opportunity" (*aphormê*), not for the "flesh" (*sarx*), but to "serve one another through love." It is important to understand that "flesh" is not simply the physical body, but the whole person turned away from God. "Self-indulgence" gives us a good sense of what Paul means by "flesh." If we do not serve the flesh, we can begin to serve God and one another.

The "you" is plural in this passage and so refers to the all of the Galatian churches, not just individuals. This is Paul's pastoral instruction for the whole church to turn away from the flesh and "serve one another through love." In fact, the verb translated "serve" here (*douleō*) is more literally "enslave." Paul's contrast between "freedom for Christ" and "slavery to flesh" is intentional: when there is properly enacted freedom in Christ, the church willingly serves each other through love (*agapê*).

When have you experienced spiritual freedom through serving others? When have you been able to move from "I" to "We"?

14 For the whole law is fulfilled in one statement, namely, "You shall love your neighbor as yourself." 15 But if you go on biting and devouring one another, beware that you are not consumed by one another.

This leads to an important verse in Galatians. When Paul says that the law is "fulfilled," he is making an important theological point. Whenever Paul speaks of Christians positively with respect to the law, he says that they "fulfill" the Law of Moses, never that they "do" it. But what does it mean that the "whole law" is "fulfilled" through love of neighbor? Since Christ has brought the law to fulfillment (Rom 10:4), Christians are now capable of living out the dictates of the law through the guidance of the Holy Spirit.

Paul only offers Leviticus 19:18 ("You shall love your neighbor as yourself") as the fulfillment of the Law, not Deuteronomy 6:4 (which enjoins the love of the one, true God), which is also the case in Romans 13:8-10. Why does Paul do this? Perhaps Paul assumes that the love of neighbor, which can be seen in word and deed, makes manifest the love of God. Paul believes

How have you been living out love of neighbor and love of God on a daily basis? Are there areas of your life that need attention to increase in love?

that the application of love in each ongoing situation in the lives of the church and of individuals, under the guidance of Christ and the Spirit, will lead people to the love of God.

Paul then admonishes the Galatians, in light of the broken relationship between Paul and the community in particular, and perhaps factions within the Galatian churches, not to "eat each other up." He uses evocative images of biting, tearing, and consuming to make his point that when we turn from love of each other, we become destroyers of each other, seeking the ruin of others and leading to the destruction of community.

16 I say, then: live by the Spirit and you will cer-
tainly not gratify the desire of the flesh. 17 For the
flesh has desires against the Spirit, and the Spirit against the flesh; these are opposed to each other, so that you may not do what you want.
18 But if you are guided by the Spirit, you are not under the law.

Paul brings us back to the image of the "flesh" and living to gratify its desires and contrasts it with living by the Spirit. "Spirit" and "flesh" are opposed forces, one leading to the ways of God, the other to self-indulgence. Indeed, Paul presents an image of the flesh having desires "against the Spirit," while the Spirit has desires "against the flesh." Whenever we wonder whether we should behave in a certain way, or do something, we need to ask whether we are satisfying the flesh or satisfying the Spirit.

If you are satisfying the Spirit, you are not "under the law." We have already seen, though, that Paul is not giving Christians license to do whatever they want when he speaks of freedom. Not to be "under the law" means that one has submitted to a different authority, for those in Christ, guided by the Spirit, "fulfill" the law. This does not mean that things are "easier," but that Christians must go beyond what is merely allowed or required by the law. As Christians we must walk the extra mile, do the extra thing, which might not be legally required, in order to show God's love to our neighbors.

Christians must go beyond what is merely allowed or required by the law.

Sometimes it seems that following the rules is the extent of what is required of us in our lives. How can you go beyond a checklist of concerns to demonstrate your love for others?

[19] **Now the works of the flesh are obvious: im-**
morality, impurity, licentiousness, [20] idolatry,
sorcery, hatreds, rivalry, jealousy, outbursts of
fury, acts of selfishness, dissensions, factions,
[21] occasions of envy, drinking bouts, orgies, and
the like. I warn you, as I warned you before, that
those who do such things will not inherit the
kingdom of God.

It is a fair question to ask, though, how does one know if we are following the Spirit? Paul initially outlines a negative path, by offering a list of the works of the flesh and so delineating those things that are opposed to the Spirit's guidance. Read the list carefully; there is something there that hits home for all of us individually, in our families or friend groups, or for our parish community. Notice that the works of the flesh listed are not just sexual sins, though they certainly appear ("impurity, licentiousness . . . orgies"), but examples of how we treat each other ("hatreds, rivalry, jealousy, outbursts of fury, acts of selfishness, dissensions, factions") and activities that substitute a god for the one, true God ("idolatry, sorcery"). The list of works of the flesh could be expanded, it seems, forever, as Paul ends with "and the like," meaning "things like I just mentioned." The works of the flesh can be multiplied in numerous ways, and so we must always be on guard that even if we are avoiding certain works of the flesh, we are not engaging in something else. "Occasions of envy" might not be as obvious as "drinking bouts" to those around us but they are indications of a war within us.

Are you struggling with particular works of the flesh? Is there someone who can give you spiritual guidance and support, such as your pastor or another professional or friend?

As a pastor and spiritual guide, Paul offers the Galatians and us a wake-up call: we can be disinherited from the kingdom of God if we do not live according to the Spirit. It's a hard reality to consider. The language of "inheritance" is significant and sometimes overlooked in Paul's letters (see, for instance, 1 Cor 6:10). It is a key image of ancient family and covenantal membership. Inheritance refers to those who are part of the family. To be a part of the family of Abraham, through the son Jesus Christ, is to be an inheritor of the kingdom. If the community, or an individual, does not behave according to the guidance of the Spirit, they can also be disinherited.

This is the equivalent of Paul as the spiritual father warning us, "You can also be asked to leave the family" or motivating us to return to the family of God.

**22 In contrast, the fruit of the Spirit is love, joy,
peace, patience, kindness, generosity, faithfulness,
23 gentleness, self-control. Against such there is
no law. 24 Now those who belong to Christ
[Jesus] have crucified their flesh with its passions
and desires. 25 If we live in the Spirit, let us also
follow the Spirit. 26 Let us not be
conceited, provoking one another, envious of one another.**

Paul encourages and exhorts us to choose a different path. What does the path of love in action look like within the family of Jesus Christ according to Paul? Christians must show evidence of the fruit of the Spirit, through simple virtues of living in love, such as joy, self-control, and gentleness. Paul says, perhaps with a smile or a wink, "there is no law against such things." While the works of the flesh are manifold, the Christian life must show evidence of the Spirit in particular virtues. Here we have a major clue as to what a life of love and the guidance of the Spirit will actually look like in practice.

How is the fruit of the Spirit most manifest in your life? Do you see these characteristics as gifts that you can offer to the church? How might you share this fruit more widely?

In a powerful phrase, Paul says the Spirit-driven life has "crucified" the flesh and its passions and desires. Remember, though, that "passions and desires" can manifest themselves in anger, cruelty, lack of concern for others, mean words, and lack of attention for those suffering, as well as partying, sexual excesses, and those things that attract more attention and censure. To live in the Spirit is to follow the Spirit and the life of the Spirit will bear fruit! Simple, but tough when we get down to the nitty-gritty of daily life. It is fascinating that when Paul speaks of "passions and desires," he speaks of ruptures in interpersonal relationships (conceit, provoking one another, and envy). In the Christian family, Paul speaks the language of love guided by the Spirit, which is the language of living together in peace.

Praying the Word / Sacred Reading

Return to the passage in Galatians 5:13-26, reading it slowly and prayerfully. Consider what words or phrases stand out for you and spend some time reflecting on why these words are speaking to you. Try to imagine yourself as a recipient of this letter from Paul in the twenty-first century in Galatians. Consider how God is speaking to you.

If you are sharing this with a group allow for some time to read the passage silently. At that point you might want one person to read the reflections below while the others consider the questions quietly. Then take time to talk about the various pieces of the passage that stand out for you.

As a part of the Galatian churches, you have found yourselves torn between what it means to truly follow Christ. Some people have said it just means following a bunch of rules. Paul the apostle has challenged you to recognize freedom in Christ. This does not mean, he says, that following Jesus is easy, or some kind of moral free-for-all, but that in Christ the Spirit guides you to love one another and to love God.

Paul not only talked about the fruit of the Spirit in his letter, but he gave an example of a Spirit-filled life by living it. The fruit of the Spirit demonstrates God's love in concrete ways regardless of the person or the situation to which they are responding.

Love, joy, peace, patience, kindness, generosity, faithfulness, gentleness, and self-control. These are the products of love of neighbor and love of God. Which of the fruits listed have you been most successful in growing? Which of these do you need to continue to cultivate? Do you need to prune back some branches to let true and new growth occur?

Perhaps the pruning has to take place in letting go of some of the works of the flesh. Is it anger? Pettiness? Sexual addictions? Too much drinking? Splitting off into factions? Do a searching inventory and pray to let go of what has been hampering your life in the Spirit. Sometimes the works of the flesh manifest themselves in withdrawal from the family of God, closing us off to the gifts and the grace of the Holy Spirit. The Spirit and the flesh are opposed to one another, Paul says, so to turn away from the flesh is to turn to the guidance of the Spirit and to a fulfillment of the law in Jesus Christ.

Living the Word

- *How might you individually, as a family, as a group or a parish truly focus on the fruit of the Spirit?*
- *Among the fruit listed, is there something that is most necessary for your parish church family at this time?*
- *How could you help guide others to grow this fruit and how might you help them walk away from the works of the flesh?*
- *Make a commitment to share in the pastoral responsibility of growing your community in the Spirit that flows into love of neighbor.*